W9-AUI-300

THE OPEN MEDIA PAMPHLET SERIES

THE OPEN MEDIA PAMPHLET SERIES

A Sustainable Economy FOR THE 21st Century

JULIET SCHOR

Series editors Greg Ruggiero and Stuart Sahulka

SEVEN STORIES PRESS / New York

A Seven Stories Press First Edition,
published in association with Open Media.

Open Media Pamphlet Series editors,
Greg Ruggiero and Stuart Sahulka.

Library of Congress Cataloging-in-Publication Data

Schor, Juliet.
    A sustainable economy for the 21st century /
Juliet Schor.
        p. cm. —(The Open Media Pamphlet Series #7)
        ISBN 1-888363-75-4 (pbk.)
        1. Sustainable development. I. Title. II. Title: A
sustainable economy for the twenty-first century.
III. Series.
HC79.E5 S2915 1998
338.9—dc21   97-51798
                                          CIP

Book design by Cindy LaBreacht

9 8 7 6 5 4 3 2 1   —

Printed in the U.S.A.

INTRODUCTION

It is Autumn 1998. Turmoil and uncertainty are in the air: the Congress is considering impeachment, the economies of Asia, Russia and Latin America have collapsed, the U.S. stock market has plunged about 20% in the last few weeks, and the danger of nuclear war has escalated dramatically. By the time this pamphlet is published, any number of national or global crises may have erupted. Or we may continue to muddle through without a full global economic collapse, but with that ever-present possibility. Meanwhile, the continued growth of the U.S. economy sustains a public complacency which at times can feel eerie. However, the fact that economy is still growing is pointed to by advocates of the so-called free market economy. This group, which includes most of the leaders of both political parties, the Beltway punditocracy, and a majority of professional economists, now virtually monopolizes the global discourse about economic issues.

Their view, the current "conventional wisdom," is that the rightward turn of the country has borne abundant fruit. This has been an unusually long expansion, prompting fantasies that the business cycle is tamed forever. Inflation remains low, despite rapid economic growth and the tightening of labor markets in the last few years. Budget surpluses have arrived. Profitability has boomed, and with it stock values, creating immense paper, and in some cases realized, wealth. Consumption has skyrocketed, as households splurge on housing, autos, travel, recreation, and many other expenditures. American corporations are "back on top," beating out competitors around the globe. As Europe remains mired in a "socialistic" malaise, and Asia in financial collapse, this country is dynamic, entrepreneurial, and confident. Even intractable problems like "welfare" have been deemed solved by "personal responsibility" and tough action by government.

The unconventional, and I think far more perceptive wisdom, is that the prosperity of some has been bought on the backs of others. "The economy" isn't doing well, wealthier households are. "Consumption" isn't booming, luxury buying is. The stock market isn't vindicating "people's capitalism"—it's enriching the portfolios of the still-small minority which holds the vast majority of the nation's financial assets. The free market is "working" for those in certain jobs, certain industries, with certain degrees, and certain backgrounds. Giving corporations a free hand has yielded, predictably, a society with far more inequality and insecurity, heightening social cleavages, and a political process which is increasingly rotten to the core. Perhaps the most stunning indictment against the pro-market interpretation is that while the Gross National Product continues to rise, measures of the Quality of Life, or Social Health, have moved in an opposite direction for two decades. We may be getting richer, on average, but overall, things look worse.[1]

What the conventional wisdom typically ignores is how narrowly the gains of this expansion have been spread. Inequality of income and wealth, which began to increase in the mid-1970s, has not improved during the 1990s. In the past, economic growth narrowed differentials. That has not yet happened. Gains remain confined to certain segments of the population. According to the latest available data (1996), the share of income going to the bottom fifth (3.8%) is lower today than when Clinton took office, and the top fifth has raised its share substantially, to nearly half of all income (49%). In dollar terms, this translates into a mere $8,596 earned by the poorest 20% of the population, as compared to the top fifth's six figure plus annual income ($115,514 to be exact). Over the long haul, the trends are similar. Since 1969, the bottom half of all households experienced virtually no increase in their median income, while the top half gained about 25%. The average income of that bottom half, at $18,000 per year, is not sufficient for a decent standard of living. By comparison, the top half earns much more—$76,000. However, even within the top half, a similar process has occurred, as gains have gone disproportionately to the better off.[2]

The inequalities of income do mask some common experiences. Even for those households with adequate incomes, the price extracted by their corporate employers has risen. Annual hours of work have grown dramatically in the last two decades, from1,745 in

8

1979 to 1,868 in 1996.[3] (And this increase is an underestimate, because it includes workers who are involuntarily working part-time.) With more people working, the squeeze on family and personal time has become intense. Jobs are more insecure and more stressful.

Other aspects of the conventional wisdom are equally dubious. It takes no great talent, or legislative reform, to reduce welfare rolls when labor markets are tightening. What is trickier is to reduce the poverty rate (hasn't happened), or keep people permanently self-supporting. Similarly, it's not too hard to keep measured unemployment low if an increasing fraction of high-unemployment groups (e.g., young males of color) are locked up in jail, or not counted, or discouraged from job search. Similarly, balancing the budget by failing to invest in public goods which yield long term returns is an accounting trick. **The bottom line is that it is always possible to make economic performance look good by marginalizing, disenfranchising, and then not counting a segment of people at the bottom.**

Underlying the changes of the 1990s is a fundamental rejection of an earlier era, in particular, of job structures and labor relations that some have termed a "golden age." The system of employer-employee relations which was in place for the first three decades after the Second World War brought an unusual degree of stability to a large percentage of Americans. Corporations accepted the idea that workers would share in productivity gains, and passed those gains along in annual increases in real wages. Corporations also tolerated the existence of unions, and worked with them, rather than against them. For white collar workers, and a segment of the blue collar ones as well, the corporation also maintained a tacit kind of employment security; not as extensive as that in Japan certainly, but nevertheless a quasi-permanent system of employment. The watchword in employment relations was stability.

True, this system never extended to everyone. People of color and women continued to be disproportionately represented in low-wage or so-called "secondary labor markets" with inferior wages, benefits, job security and job conditions. Nevertheless, aspects of the "golden age" system did work their way down to the secondary labor market. The point is perhaps made by contrast with what is happening today: the breakdown of the previous regime has left workers at all levels with fewer and fewer protections, less of a share in productivity gains, and with a deteriorating job situation. It's the "scramble to survive" system. And it's no surprise it is creating fear, insecurity, and anger. The destructuring of the employment system (i.e., scramble to survive) lies at the heart of the failure of economic recovery to improve the lives of *so* many Americans.

THE FAILED PROMISE OF A DEMOCRATIC ADMINISTRATION

In his first presidential campaign, Clinton adopted a slightly populist, "putting people first" theme. It spoke to the pressing needs of a population suffering from recession, income stagnation, and economic uncertainty. In office, he has instead focussed on "putting corporations first." In areas such as international trade, monetary and budgetary policy, food safety, and even the environment, corporate interests have taken priority. In some ways, the most disturbing aspect of the Clinton Adminstration's economic policy has been how little it differs from that of preceeding Republican administrations. There is now one kind of economics, and that is corporate.

In *The Work of Nations*, former Labor Secretary Robert Reich argues that our future depends on accepting and even welcoming the growth of increasing corporate power and reach, especially with multinational companies.[4] He, and the administration more generally, believes the globalization of the economy is both inevitable and positive. The best we can do is to make our country the place where corporations will want to put their corporate headquarters and hire sophisticated technological and managerial personnel. That's where the good jobs are supposed to come from. The other half of Reich's vision—the "human face" of concern for income inequality and low wages—is the half that has disappeared. In its place are solicitation of the bond market, deficit cutting, limiting welfare, and punitive approaches to crime.

While this administration purports to hold a more humane and active approach, its deeds—free trade pacts, balanced budgets,

12

opposition to welfare, minimal government assistance to those injured by market trends—belie that rhetoric. And even were the rhetoric credible, unquestioning adherence to corporate-driven growth raises a set of pressing questions. Whom does this type of growth benefit? The Clinton administration argues that the market knows best, which is to say that corporations know best. Clinton's team sees the government's proper role as aiding the aims of commercial enterprises, rather than helping to set priorities. As a result, they balk when it comes time to intervening in markets in ways that business dislikes: in the public or environmental interest. But will entrusting even more control and power to our large corporations serve the interests of the public or benefit the environment? Increased attention to international competitiveness may well further undermine our quality of life—by creating even more pressure to increase working hours, lower wages, and weaken environmental standards. The secretive and bureaucratically-dominated World Trade Organization has already proved disastrous to environmental, labor, and social goals.[5] Maybe what we want most from our jobs are satisfying work and employment security, not the anxiety produced by an ever "freer" market.

The promise is that growth will bring new products and more of them. But will they necessarily make us better off? How important are HDTV, computer-driven households, inflatable sneakers and yet another silk blouse? Are we still finding happiness in the consumerist lifestyle? Might we not be better served by upgrading the quality of public goods, such as schools, parks, and culture? Perhaps what we want is more time to be with our children, safer streets, better schools, and environmental preservation. The resumption of high levels of industrial growth will also intensify ecological contamination, imbalance, and decay.

The debate between Republicans and Democrats on economics has narrowed to a marginal one. Both sides now worship at the altar of the market, differing mainly on whether it should be marginally regulated in the public interest or not regulated at all. Both defend the sanctity of the existing distribution of income, wealth and power. And both Republicans and Democrats turn their backs on democracy to genuflect to the twin Gods of "growth" and "free trade." We think we've got a better idea.

THE NEW PARTY'S VISION OF A 21ST CENTURY ECONOMY

The New Party has an optimistic economic vision. We want to transform the economy in such a way that it is finally responsive, not to concentrations of wealth and power, but to the needs of ordinary people. Why this optimism at a time when the corporate steamroller appears to have virutally eliminated any opposition to "free market capitalism," when inequality continues to increase with scant public protest, and when corporate dominance of government often seems unshakeable?

Our optimism stems in part from an assessment of public opinion. Large majorities of people care about problems which cannot be solved with existing approaches. They articulate a set of basic values which are at odds with current Republican/Democratic policies and economic outcomes. Americans want a healthy, clean environment, and laws that protect the land, air, and water. Americans have a strong sense of fairness and equity. They do not believe they should be slaves to their jobs. They put peace, meaningful work, and basic values above affluence. We read the evidence as saying that people want a decent quality of life and they do not want to pay the price that global capitalism is exacting.

Any form of economy should be subject to the requirement of providing a good quality of life for all Americans in an ecologically sustainable way. That means reasonable employment security, security in material standard of living, viable family and community life, and environmental sustainability. The New Party believes that Americans can design a set of economic policies which can achieve these goals—based on principles of sustainability, democratic control, equality, and efficiency.

1. ENVIRONMENTAL SUSTAINABILITY. Year by year, the environment becomes more degraded. We are fiddling while Rome burns. If current trends continue, we may find that it is too late to save the planet from wholesale ecological deterioration. Relying on the market—economists' preference—will not work. If we contaminate and despoil the planet today, the costs will be borne by our children and grandchildren, who have no voice in today's decisions. Nor can we assume, as the Administration sometimes implies, that environmental regulations will be costless. The tradeoffs are real: autos versus clean air, housing development versus habitat preservation, nuclear power versus an unradiated biosystem, meat-centered diets versus sustainable soil and water use. We cannot continue to think about economics and the environment separately. We need to develop new ways of living and to encourage them *now* through education, debate, institutional restructuring, and democratic policy. Neither life, nor liberty, nor the pursuit of happiness are possible on a diseased and dying planet.

2. DEMOCRATIC CONTROL OF THE ECONOMY. The salient principle driving economic decisions is that money talks. This is true for the corporations who relocate plants at a moment's notice, leaving communities high and dry. It is true in the financial sector where buyouts and the resulting debt burdens destroy productive companies in a few short years. And it is true in the government, where the rich and powerful buy politicians who enact economic policy in their interest.

Right-wing ideology, and increasingly Democratic Party ideology, argues that the "money talks" principle is efficient, that democracy is too messy for the economy and that centralization of money and power creates good economic performance. But for almost two decades we have been ceding power and resources to corporations. They have gotten tax breaks. They have gotten regulatory relief. They have gotten cheap resources from the government. We have opened our schools and cultural institutions to corporate propaganda. The influence of unions has been nearly eliminated. Despite all these concessions, long-term economic performance continues to deteriorate. We might have saved ourselves the trouble by looking at the many examples of successful economies (Western Europe, Japan and Korea) in which business is more tightly regulated and controlled. It's time we read the handwriting on the wall: giving more power to business is not the way to cure the nation's ills. If the economy is to serve the people, it needs to be controlled by the people.

3. EGALITARIANISM. The U.S. economy is structured by hierarchy and inequality. In the labor market, arbitrary and rapidly changing patterns of job loss, wage reduction, and access to working hours have created new sources of inequality and insecurity. Inequality still reigns in many families, where the revolution in gender relations is far from complete. (Despite egalitarian ideologies, women still do most of the childcare and household work, even if they have jobs. And women are still responsible for children, despite their significantly lower incomes.) The global distribution of wealth and resources heavily favors the industrialized North, which has a standard of living many times that of the South. And these poor countries have been funnelling capital to the rich ones for more than a decade, causing untold misery and degradation among the poor.

In the end, everyone loses from inequalities. Corporations suffer because the talents of the people below are wasted. Workers suffer stress because they are over-supervised. More egalitarian families are better for both women, children and men. And with a more equal global economy, jobs in the industrialized countries will be less in jeopardy from low-wage competition. We believe that any truly progressive economic policy must put a very high priority on the elimination of arbitrary inequalities based on sex, race and ethnicity, sexual preference, and nation.

4. EFFICIENCY. Progressive economists have been dramatically outgunned in recent years, as the economic discourse has lurched to the right. Part of the problem is that we have clung to outdated paradigms. The Keynesian approach of big government redistributing the fruits of growth is no longer credible. We need to abandon the old tradeoff between efficiency and equality for a new vision of economic activity. We must begin by restoring nature, rather than stripping and looting it. We need to support a new business paradigm which is participatory, economically and socially responsible, flexible, and forward looking. We need to identify and articulate new efficiencies which will make a democratic economy actually work. We need reform of corporations to

JULIET SCHOR

make them less top-heavy and more accountable. We need more democratic control of government spending, and re-regulation of the
financial sector. We need to solve social problems in cost-effective ways (e.g., by prevention
rather than after-the-fact-intervention). We
need to be for change, but in a way that guarantees people security.

TIME, WORK AND MONEY: CREATING QUALITY OF LIFE

The problem of time is central to the deterioration of this nation's quality of life. The
American worker has been working a pro-
gressively longer schedule for twenty-five
years, with increases in overtime, moon-
lighting, weekly hours, weeks of work each
year, and a dramatic decline in vacations and
paid holidays. Compared to the late nineteen
sixties, the average worker is working about
an extra month of work per year. The U.S.
experience stands in sharp contrast to Western Europe, where workers enjoy four to six
week paid vacations, and declining weekly
hours. Fifty years ago the United States had

substantially shorter hours than Europe. Today, we stand with Japan as the world's workaholics.

Most economists explain these trends by people's desire to consume more, failing to see the complex forces which are leading to longer hours. Americans are working more in large part because employers are not making it possible to do otherwise. Downsizing, falling real wages, fierce competition for jobs, mandatory overtime, and a lack of decent "short hour jobs" have all contributed to the phenomenon of "the overworked American." Families are experiencing a sharp time squeeze, as the hours of both men and women rise. There's no one left to watch the children, cook the dinner, or clean the house. The rich can hire servants. But for almost everyone else, the expansion of worktime is taking its toll. Our economic program needs to give people control over their time. And we can do that.

1. NEW WORK SCHEDULES. Part of the worktime problem is that we are still operating with a "male" model of employment—full-time hours and full-time dedication to the job. A take-it-or-leave-it option. As women have entered the workforce in large numbers, they have had to conform to this model to succeed. But this causes serious problems, because women still retain primary responsibility for and attachment to child care and household work. And increasingly, men want time off the job too, often to be with their children. (If they had enough money to live as comfortably as they'd like, only 23% of adults say they would work full time, with 29% choosing part-time work, 19% volunteer work, and 25% work at home caring for family.)[6]

One solution to the time problem is to use productivity growth to reduce hours. Rather than automatically channeling productivity growth into higher wages and salaries, as they have done for 50 years, employers should give workers the option of taking shorter schedules. Through a combination of regulations and tax incentives, employers can be induced to offer worktime options, such as the choice of trading off income for time, job-sharing, the upgrading of part-time work. In addition, the Fair Labor Standards Act (FLSA) should be amended to prohibit mandatory overtime, to forbid discrimination in pay and promotion to workers who choose to work short hours, to substitute compensated time for overtime premia, to include salaried workers, and to give all American workers a guaranteed four week vacation. Over time, these measures will undermine the increasingly archaic divide between full and part-time work. Employees will be able to make their own choices about the number of hours they work without undue job and career penalties. And as a society, it will be possible for us to use our "productivity dividend" differently—to "buy" more time, rather than more things.

2. UNEMPLOYMENT AND WORKTIME. In the twenty-five years that worktime has been rising, so too have unemployment and underemployment. Unemployment and underemployment has been rising structurally since 1969, that is, correcting for the ups and downs of short term business cycles. In 1996, the true rate of joblessness—taking into account involuntary part-time work and discouraged workers—was 11%, in comparison to the government's "official" unemployment rate of 5.4%.[7] While the economic expansion of recent years has improved job market conditions, a large reserve of people remain marginalized and uncounted—casualties of downsizings, gloabalization and technical change, as well as a frayed unemployment insurance system.

The restructuring of the labor market has led to more temporary, contingent, and part-time jobs. Corporations attempt to pare down the number of core employees—those with full-time positions and benefits. And those who are *lucky* enough to land these precious core positions are expected to work long hours. Factory overtime has persisted for years at record-high levels. In the automobile industry, where tens of thousands of workers have been laid off, daily overtime has become standard, leading to a series of strikes against General Motors over excessive overtime. In the Detroit area the average workweek is 47.5 hours, Saturn workers have a regular 50-hour week, and in some plants, workers are doing 60 hours a week. The United Auto Workers (UAW) estimates that 59,000 automobile jobs would be created if the plants were on a 40 hour week.[8] High per person costs of fringe benefits, especially medical costs, are a big part of the problem. Those will only be solved with publically-funded health care. The Clinton plan would have made the problem worse by covering more people through their employers, instead of doing the sensible thing, which is to separate health insurance and employment altogether. (Why should GM be in the business of "selling" health insurance to its employees?)

It is now very unlikely that the U.S. economy can generate large numbers of jobs without reducing the hours associated with each job. The measures advocated above (especially job sharing, trading income for time, guaranteed vacations, and the abolition of mandatory overtime) should have a major impact on job creation. Beyond this, we need special attention to the high unemployment found in inner cities and in some regions of the country. We advocate two approaches: government subsidies for job creation among groups and geographical areas with high unemployment rates and direct employment programs by local governments.

3. CONSUMERISM, THE ENVIRONMENT AND THE PRODUCTIVITY DIVIDEND. Looking back over the past fifty years, the U.S. experience raises troubling questions. We have more than doubled our productive potential, as a result of rising productivity. Had we channeled this "productivity dividend" into leisure time, Americans would have already reached the twenty hour week. But instead we used all of our economic progress to produce more goods and services, and to consume more. So Americans of all income classes got a higher material standard of living—about twice as "high"—but not many got more leisure time. On the contrary, those of us with jobs have lengthened our hours.

We have gotten more things, but there is growing evidence that consumerism is not giving us satisfaction and peace of mind. Americans are neither happier nor more satisfied. Measures of social health show decline, not progress. Millions feel trapped in a cycle of working and spending, running faster and staying in place. Might it not be time to hop off that treadmill? As a society, we have achieved affluence as measured by average income; nonetheless, an increasing number of Americans are impoverished. But if we choose, which we should, to distribute our wealth more equitably, everyone in this country could live well, indeed handsomely, by historical comparison. Even for those who have achieved a middle class standard of living, quality of life is problematic. Now it's time to figure out how the consumerist lifestyle relates to true well-being.

One thing we do know is that consumerism is disastrous for the environment. The last half-century of growth has been the most ecologically destructive in human history, and the United States, with its big malls, fast food, and lots of private (versus public consumption) has developed the most ecologically damaging pattern of consumption in the world. How can we reconcile our needs for material comfort, adequate time, and a healthy planet?

A SUSTAINABLE ENVIRONMENT

Economic activity must become sustainable. This will involve new ways of living. There are areas of waste (packaging, failure to conserve energy), which need to be eliminated. The U.S.

military, the world's single-largest polluter, must be brought under control. Nuclear power must be eliminated and the environment spared from more radioactive waste. Much environmental degradation can be prevented by changing our basic systems of production and consumption. On the production side, factories and offices have been built and designed with the assumption of free or low-cost natural resources. We need to move to closed-loop systems, where waste, toxic chemicals, radioactive materials, and pollution resources are not produced in the first instance. On the consumption side, we need to design new systems of housing and transport. Although these prescriptions may sound politically infeasible today, we believe there is a strong reservoir of support for sustainability. In a 1995 poll 37% of respondents strongly agreed and 40% agreed somewhat that "American over-use of resources is a major global environmental problem that needs to be changed."[9]

1. GREEN QUOTAS AND TAXES. As we destroy more and more of the planet's clean air, water, habitats, and ecosystems, the underpricing of these resources becomes an increasingly calamitous practice. We need an economic system which values natural capital, in addition to physical, financial, and human capital. First, we propose incorporating natural resource accounting into the Gross National Product. (A preliminary step has recently been taken in this direction, which we applaud.) This would provide the basis for setting limits or quotas on polluting and degrading production activities. For example, industries would be restricted to producing fixed amounts of toxic wastes, airborne or waterborne pollutants. On the consumption side, we advocate the introduction of a national value-added "green" tax. This tax would be levied on consumers at the retail level, so that they pay the true social costs of their consumption activities. Examples of commodities which might be taxed are gasoline; household, lawn and pool chemicals; air conditioners; meat; furniture; jet travel; and disposable products. The tax should be clearly identified, so that consumers are informed about the environmental consequences of their purchases.

2. INDUSTRY-WIDE ENVIRONMENTAL STAN-DARDS. One barrier to sustainable practices is competition among businesses. If every toothpaste manufacturer feels a cardboard box is necessary to entice the consumer to buy, moral appeals to reduce packaging will not be powerful. By contrast, industry-wide standards have the potential to reduce costs without adversely affecting individual producers. We propose the introduction of industry-wide standards in areas such as packaging; energy efficiency for appliances, heating units, vehicles; and household construction.

3. ALTERNATIVE HOUSING AND TRANS-PORTATION. A key environmental problem is that current systems of housing and transport are unsustainable. In American suburbia, houses are large and costly to build. They are energy inefficient and cannot be kept cool without air conditioning. They have large lawns, often with ecologically destructive landscaping. Because of the distances and the land-use patterns, automobile travel (extremely damaging) is virtually imperative. Sprawl is destroying habitats and eco-systems. We need to initiate a long-term shift to smaller, differently designed houses, with new transportation systems and new conceptions of land use. Ultimately, we believe these changes will improve the quality of life as well. With mixed land-use patterns, people can work, shop and live in a close geographic area, a lifestyle we believe is becoming increasingly popular. Walking, bicycling, and public transportation become feasible. Community is easier to maintain. And, in this era of time-stressed, dual-earner couples, freedom from the large time commitment required for maintaining suburban homes and lifestyles will be increasingly appealing to people.

RESTRUCTURING THE ENTERPRISE

Our major economic problem is not the government, as conservatives claim, but the American enterprise itself. GM and IBM are only the most visible examples of how this once mighty institution has gone awry. Large U.S. corporations became arrogant, complacent, and unresponsive. They are not rooted in basic values of accountability to people they serve—employees, consumers, communities, or stockholders. The biggest dinosaurs are crumbling before our eyes, and many more companies have serious problems.

On the other hand, small business is not a panacea. Small companies typically pay less and have fewer benefits than their larger cousins. Indeed, the problems of the enterprise may ultimately be less an issue of size than of restructuring. We need new structures of governance, new models of behavior and new sets of incentives.

1. PROMOTING SOCIAL ACCOUNTABILITY. This country already possesses a growing sector of socially innovative companies. Some are small, some large. What ties them together is that they are able to combine enviable conditions for their employees with principles of social accountability, such as environmental sustainability, community revitalization, or global equity. They subject their products to standards of social usefulness. Many are employee-owned although many have traditional ownership structures. Some of these companies are well-known, such as Ben &

Jerry's or the South Street Bank in Chicago. Together they represent a range of new models of corporate structure, behavior and performance which we need to take a careful look at.

We need to expand this sector of the economy. Government should provide strong incentives for democratically-controlled enterprises, such as consumer cooperatives, employee-owned firms, and municipally and community-owned enterprises. Examples of such incentives include tax subsidies, regulatory encouragement, financial schemes, preferential buying and technical aid. We call for the establishment of a demanding Federal code of social responsibility. Companies which abide by it should be eligible for "most favored company" status, with attendant benefits.

2. CORPORATE GOVERNANCE. The failure of corporate America is a failure of governance. Corporations are not sufficiently accountable either to their stockholders or to their "stakeholders"—the employees, customers, suppliers, and communities who comprise and depend on the corporation. We propose a comprehensive Corporate Democracy Act. Its centerpiece would be a mandate for newly constituted Boards of Directors. These would be filled from outside the ranks of management and include not only representatives of stockholders, but stakeholders as well. Directors would be elected by the various stakeholder groups. The Corporate Democracy Act would also erode the legal fiction of the corporation as person, thereby creating increased civil and criminal liability for individual managers. The Act would also transfer corporate chartering to the Federal government and set minimum standards for tax subsidies, pollution, and unfair labor practices, thereby avoiding destructive state-against-state bidding to attract investment. Finally, we call for amendment of ERISA to allow worker-owners more control over the $2 trillion of pension assets about which they currently have no say.

3. RESTRUCTURING LABOR RELATIONS. The labor market has been undergoing restructuring for over a decade. Long-term job security is being substituted with temporary and casual employment, the use of consultants, outsourcing, and a variety of other techniques which erode commitments to employees. This is the "scramble to survive" system. In this regime, productivity will be zealously monitored, pay continuously adjusted. We are told this is what is necessary to keep afloat in the global capitalist economy.

We reject the "scramble to survive" model. Not only is it inhumane, it's bad economics. Insecurity undermines efficiency. It creates stress and erodes loyalty. The dismal results from downsizings bear this out. We can do better. Our vision of restructured employment relations also contains an imperative to become more efficient, but contends that we can do so by restructuring authority relations and giving employees a genuine voice in the running of their companies.

We would begin by eliminating management layers, sharply curtailing the number of supervisory personnel, and creating new structures of power and authority. The United States has been devoting about 13.5% of its non-farm employment to administrative and managerial personnel, as compared to ratios of less than one-third that among our competitors—3.3% (France), 3.3% (Germany), 4.2% (Japan).[10]

While some of this wasteful staffing has been eliminated recently, U.S. corporations are still too top-heavy. In restructurings what matters most is how the process occurs. Simply cutting personnel, as companies have been doing, creates overwork and stress for the remaining employees. The flow of work and decision-making authority itself must change, giving more latitude to teams and people farther down the hierarchy. People must be allowed more freedom of self-management. This will reduce stress and increase productivity. Skill levels will rise—one requirement for the twenty-first century economy everyone can agree upon. The millions of workers whose skills are already under-utilized will have a chance to see what they can do.

Ultimately, employees can only be "empowered" (another contemporary buzz-word) if they have organizations through which to exercise their voices.[11] The precipitous decline of union membership means that U.S. workers are now virtually unrepresented, despite the fact that polls show a significant unmet demand both for unions per se, and for other forms of collective representation. We propose changes in labor legislation which will increase the fraction of the workforce which belongs to unions, and foster other forms of employee organization (in both union and non-union settings). Reforms which would facilitate unionization include card check certification for the choice of bargaining representative, the legalization of minority union membership and activity, stronger penalties for employer unfair labor practices, and extension of the right to unionize into the ranks of exempt employees.

4. CHANGING CORPORATE CULTURE. Of course, most of the nation's management would be bitterly opposed to most of the afore-mentioned changes. They would see them as unworkable and disruptive. But before we let them do away with our jobs, we should assess how well they are doing theirs. Isn't their stewardship increasingly a failure? The times clearly call for innovation and change. But the so-called "pro-business" vision of change is not much more than a return to the nineteenth century—anti-union, anti-worker, anti-safety, anti-leisure mindset. Their narrowmindedness is leading them, and the nation, backwards. Let's try to take them forward, to a new democratic model of work relations and enterprise.

POVERTY AND INEQUALITY

The distribution of income in the United States is now the most unequal among the industrialized countries of the world. Between 1973 and 1996, the income share of the bottom fifth of families fell a full percentage point, from 5.5 to 4.2%. The share of the top fifth rose from 41.1% to 46.8%. The top 10% of the population now own 73% of the nation's total privately-held wealth, and wealth is also becoming more unequally distributed.

The decline in income for the bottom fifth has led to increasing rates of poverty. By official measures, 13.7% of the population was poor in 1996. But official definitions are sorely out of date; one more recent estimate puts actual poverty at one quarter of the population. Not only are there more poor people, but they are getting poorer—their incomes are falling even farther below the poverty line. More than twenty percent of all children in this country are now poor.[12]

Much of the poverty problem can be laid at the feet of sex and race discrimination. Nearly thirty-six percent of female-headed families are poor. That's largely because 40% of women earn wages (in 1997 dollars) of $8.25 an hour or less. With a 40 hour week, that's an income of only about $16,500 a year.[13] And despite all the attention to women's economic progress, these women are earning *less* per hour than they did 25 years ago. The income gains have all gone to the highly-paid. About half the nation's women workers still cannot manage a decent standard of living without the help of a man. This is a basic and sobering fact of economic life for women. The closing of the gender wage gap in the last ten years (from the famous 59 cent figure to the most recent estimate of 79 cents) has been mainly due to falling wages for men. The story is similar for racial minorities. Among African Americans, 38.2% of workers did not earn an hourly wage sufficient to lift them out of poverty. Among Hispanics, the comparable fraction was 46.7%. Affirmative action not withstanding, African Americans and Latino/-as are still concentrated in the economy's least desirable, lowest paying occupations.[14]

40

1. RAISING LOW WAGES: COMPARABLE WORTH AND THE MINIMUM WAGE. The first step to solving these problems is to recognize that they are based on an implicitly discriminatory valuation of the work that people do. Research has shown that women's work is paid less, *just because women do it.* Women and non-whites are far less rewarded for their education, skills and experience. Comparable worth programs aim to root out these often-subtle discriminations. The programs use existing compensation methods to recalibrate the worth of various jobs, in the absence of discriminatory effects. They are instituted by employers, and they have been very successful, particularly in rectifying inequities against the lowest paid, who are often employees of color. We recommend that all places of employment be required to institute comparable worth programs. We envision this being phased in over a three year period.

Although the minimum wage has been raised in recent years, the increases have been insufficient. Despite occasional political rhetoric to the contrary, almost two-thirds of minimum wage workers, are women, and the vast majority are adults. As compared to twenty years ago, the real value of the minimum wage has fallen 20%. We suggest a phased-in increase to $8.00 an hour for adults, with subsequent pegging of the minimum to the median wage in the economy. Although the conventional wisdom is that a higher minimum will cause unemployment, new evidence disputes this view. If a higher adult minimum is instituted with productivity-enhancing measures, it is affordable.

2. THINKING BIG. The 1996 welfare legislation, and the accompanying debate, with its mixture of Dickensian and Orwellian qualities, has been a sobering reminder of how close Democrats and Republicans have become. The facts and realities of welfare programs have been lost in a frenzied attack on women, people of color and the poor. But scapegoating the least powerful among us will not address the underlying dissatisfactions being pandered to by politicians. Neither will cutting welfare spending, which is quantitatively negligible.

We believe that the entire thrust of the welfare debate must be transformed. We say, let's think about "welfare" the way we think about social security. It should be a "universal entitlement": everyone contributes and everyone is eligible. This welfare program would be run with a minimum of bureaucracy—basically as a check printing service, with no social workers or administrators. It is called a Basic Income Grant (BIG), and has gained a steady following in Europe. The idea is that every citizen would be eligible to receive a minimum income from the government, which would be sufficient to provide a modest standard of living. A BIG would allow people to opt out of the labor market for a while, to raise their children or pursue activities that are not lucrative (the arts, community work, or social services). It would enable them to retire when they feel ready, or to pursue schooling or retraining. Eligibility would be tied to a work requirement: the length of eligibility for receiving BIG would be tied to past work and participation in unpaid community service, as well as child and elder care.

In America, the introduction of a basic income grant would be a radical departure from historic practice. But we think it's worth beginning to think about. The likelihood of further job loss, the growing desire of people to pursue activities outside their jobs, and the crisis of inadequate family time all point to something like a BIG. As labor market status and family composition become increasingly precarious, our basic systems of providing income (income from work and income transfers within the family) are proving inadequate. We need a comprehensive social security system which guarantees stability in the face of family breakup, labor market displacement, and other unpredictable events which disrupt people's access to income. BIG could be that system. We're not sold on it. But we definitely think it should be on the table.

THE GLOBAL VILLAGE

The 21st century will make good on the promise of a global village. Communication, migration, and commerce will grow. But the global village raises the problem of inequities between countries and relations among them. Today, the United States has less than 5% of the world's population, but consumes roughly 30% of its resources. Eight percent of the world's population own cars, as compared to about 90% of Americans. The American child's annual pocket money—$230 a year—exceeds the income of the world's half-billion poorest people.[15]

The problem of global inequities is complex. On the one hand, how can the conditions of life be raised for those in poor countries? On the other, with increasing international competition, how can we in the North avoid having our living standards dragged down to the level of Mexico, Brazil or China? Progressives have argued that the answer lies in raising wage levels in places like Mexico, Brazil and China, rather than letting international competition bring down U.S. wages. Fair enough. But for environmental reasons, we cannot simply "raise living standards to our own." The earth cannot support five billion people (or twice that, by the next century) who are driving cars, eating meat, turning on the air conditioning when it gets hot, and throwing away a can every time they drink a soda. But what else have development and rising incomes meant but emulating the American way of life?

Our vision of the global economy is based on two principles. First, neither free trade nor protection is the answer. We advocate instead a world trading system whose foundation is a series of international agreements guaranteeing basic rights and protections for workers and citizens. Second, those agreements must safeguard the environmental health of a planet in a globally equitable way. Those of us in the developed world, because we account for the bulk of the world's pollution, have a special responsibility to change our lifestyles and methods of production.

1. A NEW WORLD TRADING SYSTEM. One problem with an international "free market" is that it can drag down wages, environmental regulations, and social welfare programs to the level of the worst-off country. This was the basis of much of the original opposition to NAFTA. U.S. companies can move or threaten to move their production to Mexico if American workers don't take wage cuts. Similarly, the government can be coerced into rescinding environmental regulations or social programs if employers oppose them. It becomes impossible to regulate business if capital is free to move to countries without such regulation.

On the other hand, protectionism is not the answer. Ultimately, protectionism has helped employers, not workers. Jobs are rarely saved permanently. And prices rise for consumers. Furthermore, protectionism pits U.S. workers against workers in other countries, who often want and need jobs as desperately, or more, than we do.

How can we steer our boat between the Scylla of free trade and the Charybdis of protection? We can be for world trade, but in a framework of minimum standards. Countries would have to abide by international codes of conduct on workers' rights and environmental protections which would stipulate basic protections such as minimum wages, maximum hours of work, rights to representation, and non-discrimination by race and sex, as well as the regulation of air and water emissions, toxic wastes, etc. (The green quotas and taxes we proposed above would be the national versions of such agreements.) The codes would be sensitive to the situations of poor countries, and would allow for initial differences in some of the standards to which countries are held. They would also contain provisions which allow poor countries access to "clean" technologies.

In a world trading system built on such cooperative agreements it would no longer be possible for Japan to gain advantage because workers are forced to put in unpaid overtime. Or for companies to cross the border to Mexico to avoid environmental regulations. When countries violate or refuse to sign on to these agreements, their products would be subjected to "social tariffs" which would be set to compensate for the deviation from the code. If Brazil was a dollar below the global minimum wage, a Brazilian product taking one hour to make would carry a $1.00 tariff. If Korea has cheaper steel because its plants are more polluting, or its workers get no leisure time, the social tariff would make up the difference so that the Korean steel would no longer have a cost advantage. Over time, the tariffs become a powerful incentive for companies to improve environmental performance and their treatment of employees. Where the tariff revenue goes (to the consuming country, or into a global facility) is a matter open for discussion.

If this sounds utopian, remember that the International Labour Organization has already developed codes of labor rights; the problem now is enforcement. And global environmental protections such as the Montreal Protocol and the treaties emanating from the Rio Summit are already being enacted. What is lacking is the political will and leadership to move forward.

BUDGET, TAXES AND FINANCE

So far we have said very little about the budget, taxes, and spending, an issue which dominated the economic discourse for much of the 1990s. During the years of budgetary deficit, we argued that the importance of the shortfall in the government account was overstated. Indeed, when properly calculated, the deficit was far smaller than was commonly recognized. Now that the budget has been balanced, we need to remember that conservatives have used the deficit as a political ruse, to cut social spending they do not like. We believe that structurally, budget balance is a reasonable goal, but we oppose cuts in social spending in the name of deficit reduction. And likewise, we believe that any budget surpluses should be used to address basic needs in areas such as housing, education, health, child care and the like. We cannot forget that budget balance has been achieved on the backs of the poor, middle classes, and others of limited political clout.

1. TAX REFORM. Despite all the talk of tax and spend Democrats, the fraction of national income going to Federal taxes has only risen slightly since 1973.[16] However, regressive payroll taxes have taken up a larger share than the more progressive income tax. And the corporate tax burden has fallen significantly. State and local taxes, comprised largely of the more regressive sales and property taxes, have risen. We believe that continued reform of the tax system is necessary, both to continue the path to simpler taxes and to create a fairer tax system. We advocate reinstating progressive measures into the tax system. For Federal income taxes these include the expansion of exemptions at lower income levels and higher rates at the top; eliminating income caps for payroll taxes; and bringing corporate profits back into the taxation system. At the state and local levels we advocate greater reliance on income taxes. We also propose much higher inheritance taxes, so that unfair economic advantage does not carry through from generation to generation.

2. REDUCING FEDERAL SPENDING. Like many conservatives, we favor reduced Federal spending. But we believe in military downsizing, cutting subsidies to agribusiness and fossil-fuel and nuclear energy sources, and reduced interest payments to wealthy bondholders. In conjunction with the tax reforms we advocated above, these changes will bring down the Federal deficit. We advocate splitting the federal accounts into consumption and investment components. In the long run, we advocate the elimination of any "structural" deficit in consumption spending. With respect to investment spending, deficits are not a problem because they generate increased revenue in future years.

3. RE-REGULATING FINANCIAL MARKETS. Neither Democrats nor Republicans now have any inclination to reassume the control over financial markets which was ceded through deregulation and the failure to keep up with innovations in finance. No surprise then, that Clinton has been the "darling" of the bond market. But pandering to the financiers will not bring us economic health. By now it is widely recognized that deregulation has had disastrous effects: the savings and loan scandals, the global financial crisis, and the growing influence, corruption, and income of financiers. The federal government, in conjunction with international regulatory agencies, needs to reassume a modicum of control over financial markets. We need reregulation to reintroduce prudence and eliminate the incentives for reckless behavior which currently exist. The principles of regulation should be that *all* financial institutions are regulated equivalently (i.e., the so-called level playing field); that regulations *raise*, not lower the field (unregulated financial institutions are a recipe for disaster); and that a financial social contract be introduced in which the privilege to be a lending institution with Federal deposit insurance carries with it responsibilities to poor and urban communities and small businesses which are starved for funds.

52

Financial reform should also address the structural position of the Federal Reserve, which is insulated from democratic pressures and mainly accountable to large banks and financial institutions. This accountability is in large part responsible for the high real interest rates of the past decade and a half, and the attendant negative effects on investment and productivity. The Federal Reserve should be brought under more Congressional control, and appointments to the Board of Governors should be restructured to introduce citizen influence. Finally, we favor reforms which will decentralize finance, and increase availability of funds for socially worthwhile projects which traditional bankers will not support. We applaud the Clinton administration's advocacy of new, local community financing vehicles. These could be federally supported, and devoted to providing alternative sources of finance.

SOLVING THE PRODUCTIVITY PROBLEM

Many of the reforms we have been talking about will require new economic resources. Cleaning up the environment, raising the wages of the bottom half, giving ourselves more leisure time, or instituting a basic income grant are all costly proposals, in their own ways. Yet the prevailing reality is that we are living in a world of increasing scarcity of resources and that we are getting poorer, not richer.

New resources can be found by organizing our economy and society more rationally. For example, unemployment deprives the economy of the productivity of the unemployed, and creates costly social problems such as poor health, crime, and family dissolution. So too have we been dealing with crime in an inefficient way (locking people up at a great cost to society). There has been a tremendous growth of "unproductive" employees in our society (excessive numbers of paper-pushers, supervisors, and security guards). A more equitable and participatory economy could do away with many of these functions, thereby freeing up resources. But ultimately, new resources will have to be created through productivity growth: becoming more efficient in our methods of production and distribution.

The recent U.S. record on productivity growth has not been good, in comparison to our competitors. And herein lies much of the concern about the decline of the U.S. economy. Economists don't have a very good understanding of why productivity growth has been so meager, but the likely culprits are low investment, heavy-handed labor management, declining quality of education and training, the short-term perspective imposed by financial markets, distorted resource use due to uncounted environmental costs, and a long start-up period for new technologies. We also believe that the growing inequities of our society are having an impact: unemployment, poor schools, crime, drugs, homelessness. All these problems take their toll.

Productivity growth in manufacturing has been far better than in services, where more than 70% of Americans are employed. The productivity problem is in many ways a service sector problem caused by low wages, high turnover, low capital intensity, low levels of education and training. Much of the service sector is an "economic backwater" in need of upgrading. The policies of the Republican administrations have encouraged low-wage, low-cost labor, allowing businesses to get by without investing in new technologies or organizational innovations. We need policies which stimulate innovation, technical change, and upgrading. We need to encourage (or force) companies to invest in their employees' "human capital," knowing that when they do, they are paid back handsomely. In a global economy, to do otherwise is to court disaster. If we do not raise our productiveness in services, our wage levels *will* be dragged down the international scale, from Britain to Spain to Turkey and finally Mexico and Brazil.

Many of the reforms mentioned above will help, such as comparable worth and raising the minimum wage. So too will reform of labor relations. We also advocate the maintenance of a highly-valued dollar, rather than allowing continued depreciation. Similarly, we need federal help in upgrading public schools and a comprehensive program to make college educations available and affordable for all. And we also need direct incentives (for example, loan programs and tax credits) for service sector businesses, particularly small ones. Government could institute tax reductions for companies which achieve high productivity growth, thereby encouraging the most productive businesses and penalizing the least.

These ideas rest on the historical evidence that there are two paths to economic growth. One is the high-wage, high-productivity route. The other is with low-wages, least-costs, and low productivity. This country got rich with the first, and is now getting poor with the second. We think it's time to change that.

ECONOMIC POLICY IN THE AGE OF GLOBALIZATION

Looking over the economic policy debates of the past fifteen years, the steady demise of progressive economic ideas is striking. A Democratic President dares not even speak out for strong side agreements on labor and environment in NAFTA, regulation of financial markets, or an effective approach to joblessness. This is a measure of how narrow and corporate-dominated the economic discourse has become. The absence of a progressive voice is in no small part due to the powerlessness that people feel in the context of a globalizing economy. We have been taught—by liberal Democrats and Republicans alike—that our nation is *subject to* global trends, not a creator of them. We have been taught that other nations, especially Japan, cause our economic problems. And we have been taught that the "free market" is the only rational economic institution available to us.

These views are ideology, not reality. They represent the interests of the world's most powerful economic actors, the large transnational corporations who are making an increasingly successful bid to free themselves from even modest levels of social accountability. If it did nothing else, the fight over NAFTA identified whose interests lie where. Globalization is mainly a process being carried out by the giant transnationals, among whom the U.S. players are the most numerous and powerful. If ordinary people and national governments are becoming powerless in the face of globalization, it is because we are ceding that power to our own corporations. The market is not impersonal, it is not too big to regulate, and most of all it is not free. It is created and maintained by concentrations of corporate and gov-

JULIET SCHOR

ernmental power. Our urgent task in the area of economics is to confront the myth of economic impotence perpetuated by America's archaic political system, and to mobilize alternative visions for a sustainable economy in the 21st century. I hope that this pamphlet contributes to that goal.

NOTES

1. On wider measures, see the Geniune Progress Indicator of the Redefining Progress group in San Francisco, or the Social Health Index, of Fordham University.

2. Income distribution data from Census Bureau, Report on Income Inequality, June 17, 1996. Table 2. These estimates rely on official estimates of the Consumer Price Index, which may, however, overstate inflation.

3. On annual hours, see Mishel, Bernstein, and Schmitt, 1998. Table 3.1, p.123.

4. For an exposition of this view, see Robert Reich, *The Work of Nations*, (New York: Knopf, 1991).

5. For an excellent discussion of GATT, and the global economy more generally, see Jerry Mander and Edward Goldsmith, eds, *The Case Against the Global Economy* (San Francisco: Sierra Club Books) 1996.

6. The Harris Poll, May 10, 1992, #26.

7. On Joblessness, see Ward Morehouse and david dembo, *Joblessness: The Underbelly of the U.S. Economy*, 1997 (New York: Apex Press).

8. For Detroit figure and jobs estimates, see "Overtime: Dangerous to Our Children and Communities," Dave Yettaw, *The Voice of New Directions* newsletter, UAW National Edition, vol. 6, #2, June 1994, p. 1. For 60 hour figure see "Forced Overtime: Killing the American Dream," *New Directions*, undated.

9. Global Stewardship Initiative, Pew Foundation, Poll. Unpublished results, 1994.

10. David M. Gordon, "The Bureaucratic Burden in the Advanced Economies: A Cross–National Perspective on Monitoring and Supervision," *American Economic Review, Papers and Proceedings*, May 1994, Table 1.

11. See for example, Richard B. Freeman and Joel Rogers, "Who Speaks for Us?," in Bruce E. Kaufman and Morris N. Kleiner, eds. *Employee Representation: Alternatives and Future Directions*, (Madison, WI: Industrial Relations Research Association,) 1993.

12. Income distribution data from Lawrence Mishel, Jared Bernstein, and John Schmitt, *The State of Working America*, (Economic Policy Institute and M.E. Sharpe, 1998). Family distribution of income, Table 1.6, p. 49; wealth distribution, Table 5.5, p. 262; poverty rates, Tables 6.1 and 6.3, pps. 257, 279, 281.

13. Mishel and Bernstein, and Schmitt, 1998. Poverty and female-headed families, Table 6.15, p.298; Wages, Table 3.8, p. 138.

14. Mishel, Bernstein, and Schmitt, 1998. Gender wage gap, Table 3.9, p. 135. Between 1989 and 1997, 74.4% of the change was due to lower male wages. For Blacks and Hispanics, Tables 3.12 and 3.13, pps. 141-142.

15. Statistics from "All–Consuming Passion: Waking Up from the American Dream," New Road Map Foundation, Seattle, Washington, 1993, pps. 10–11.

16. Mishel, Bernstein, and Schmitt, 1998, p.92.

JULIET SCHOR is the author of the best-selling book, *The Overworked American: The Unexpected Decline of Leisure* (Basic Books 1992) and *The Overspent American: Upscaling, Downshifting and the New Consumer* (Basic Books 1998). Schor earned her B.A. from Wesleyan University and her Ph.D. in economics from the University of Massachusetts at Amherst. She has been teaching at Harvard University since 1984, where she is currently a Senior Lecturer on Women Studies. She lives in Newton, Mass with her husband and two children. Schor originally wrote this pamphlet in the summer of 1995 for the New Party. This edition contains a new introduction and some updating throughout the text.

OTHER OPEN MEDIA PAMPHLET SERIES TITLES AVAILABLE

CORPORATE MEDIA AND THE
THREAT TO DEMOCRACY
Robert W. McChesney
80 pages / $5.95 / ISBN: 1-888363-47-9

MEDIA CONTROL: THE SPECTACULAR
ACHIEVEMENTS OF PROPAGANDA
Noam Chomsky
64 pages / $5.95 / ISBN: 1-888363-49-5

GENE WARS: THE POLITICS
OF BIOTECHNOLOGY
Kristin Dawkins
64 pages / $4.95 / ISBN: 1-888363-48-7

GLOBALIZING CIVIL SOCIETY:
RECLAIMING OUR RIGHT TO POWER
David C. Korten
80 pages / $5.95 / ISBN: 1-888363-59-2

ZAPATISTA ENCUENTRO: DOCUMENTS FROM THE
1996 ENCOUNTER FOR HUMANITY AND AGAINST
NEOLIBERALISM
The Zapatistas
64 pages / $5.95 / ISBN: 1-888363-58-4

PROPAGANDA INC: SELLING AMERICA'S CULTURE
TO THE WORLD
Nancy Snow
80 pages / $5.95 / ISBN: 1-888363-74-6

TO ORDER ADDITIONAL SERIES TITLES CALL 1 (800) 596-7437.